REFLECTIVE THINKING

REFLECTIVE THINKING

Reverend Brian Branche

ATHENA PRESS
LONDON

ISBN 1 84401 570 X

First Published 2005 by
ATHENA PRESS
Queen's House, 2 Holly Road
Twickenham TW1 4EG
United Kingdom

Printed for Athena Press

Dedication

When in 1876 Mary Sumner, a Manchester-born wife of a clergyman, was inspired to create the Mother's Union in her husband's parish, little did she know that in 1885 it would become Diocesan based as it is today. No longer seen as middle-class ladies wearing flowery hats, they have moved into the twenty-first century with more than a million members in seventy countries and the largest Christian charity in the UK. The women, often with 'sleeves rolled up', are seen as front-line missionaries in Third World countries, often working in life-threatening situations with spiritual and social policies helping to 'make poverty history'.

They are the backbone of the Church if England and it is to their work that I dedicate Reflective Thinking.

Preface

Life is full of challenges, contradictions, joy, despair – the whole gamut of emotions – and Father Brian writes about all of these and more in his book, *Reflective Thinking*. A deep-thinking man, he offers his thoughts and solutions on a whole range of situations. I especially liked his prayers at the end of each chapter.

Father Brian's faith shines from each page as he constantly reminds us of the love that God has for all of us if we will only accept Him into our hearts and lives. Our faith can be our greatest tool as we strive to become better people.

This is a gem of a book, written by an inspirational man and dedicated to a worldwide organisation of inspirational women – The Mothers' Union.

I recommend it to you.

Pat Williams
Branch Leader
St Matthew's Little Lever Mothers' Union

Foreword

Faced with the world's problems it is all too easy to give up – and think, "There's nothing I can do about it." To counter that temptation, Brian Branche has written this engaging little book that offers much to ponder. He shows that the secret to discovering how each of us really can make a difference lies not so much in clever scholarship as in having a genuine interest in life.

Brian certainly has that himself. Through these pages his warm personality shines through, as he reflects on the mundane; and by homely illustrations and frequent references to scripture, encourages us to read the Bible. For, as he indicates, when we do that we discover its words are full of life. Then we ourselves become alive, and see there are things we really can do to turn problems into opportunities. I am happy to commend *Reflective Thinking* and pray that many will be helped by it.

The Right Reverend Nigel S McCulloch
Bishop of Manchester

Introduction

1

Reflective Thinking was conceived in the womb of past dreams; dreams that have played an important part in my life, helping me to come to terms with insecurity and low self-esteem in early childhood, puberty, and, as a young adult, with an inquisitive mind always wanting to know "Why do things turn out as they do?"

Dreams can be as simple or as complicated as we make them. Maybe they do not always surrender all the secrets invested in the subconscious, but they offer a morsel of information to the dreamer, whose understanding of it all is more often than not beyond comprehension, leaving one with many unanswered questions and wondering whether dreams are a fantasy.

Are dreams the fantasy of our wishful thinking, of children acting out a role as a hero or of someone who feels special? Is Christianity wishful thinking, and what about heaven and hell? Have dreams the power to stir and, if remembered, embrace an element of truth about our character? Who knows, for many a person has ridden his life on the wings of a dream to serve his God and in doing so has become his true self, like Joseph for example, becoming the father of a nation: Israel! Now, Joseph had a dream (Genesis 37:5); Mary's husband, Joseph, was also spoken to through a dream (Matthew 2:13); Pilate's wife had a dream (Matthew 27:13); old men shall dream (Acts 2:17); Nebuchadnezzar also had a dream (Daniel 2:1).

Dreams have helped fashion many a life, including mine, and maybe for me they have been like a window allowing me to glimpse that secret place we call the soul where earth and heaven meet and good and evil struggle as we try to make some sense of truth, life and death, over and against our mortality and defence-lessness as we seek to become independent and self-reliant as individuals and take our place in society.

2

The view that dreams are merely the imaginary fulfilment of repressed wishes is hopelessly out of date. There are, it is true, dreams which manifestly represent wishes or fears, but what about all the other things? Dreams may contain ineluctable truths, philosophical pronouncements. Illusions, wild fantasies, memories, plans, anticipations, irrational experiences, even telepathic visions, and heaven knows what besides.

C G Jung

Little did I know at the age of thirteen – when I dreamt I saw the face of Christ crucified (see my book *Seconds Out*, Athena Press 2005), and fell in love with the face of compassion it expressed – that love would lead me into a lifelong journey of faith, discovering the wonder and beauty of creation and the glory of God as Father, Son and Holy Spirit. Nor did I appreciate or expect that the journey of faith would not be a comfortable one, making me question the catechism I had to learn parrot-fashion while attending a Roman Catholic secondary modern school in Brighton, Sussex, which failed to exercise the muscles of faith or put flesh on dry bones (Ezekiel 37).

It was through the unusual process of dreams that I have discovered the joy and wonder of God incarnate in Christ, and not the God of schooldays, who, more often than not, put fear into our hearts with "thou shall not", rather than revealing the joy of growing up. It is one of the reasons I love reading the story of the prodigal son (Luke 15:11) for the younger son comes to appreciate his father's love after he has sowed his wild oats and spent his inheritance; something the elder son fails to acknowledge although he had been basking in the same embrace of love he is now witnessing being bestowed upon his younger brother.

3

Perhaps dry bones rest in the graveyard of faith, taking God's love for granted, and it takes the Breath of God to refresh and revitalise the soul to sing his praise in unity with the Spirit of Christ:

For He who sanctifies and those who are being sanctified are all one, for which reason He is not ashamed to call them brethren, saying 'I will declare your name to my brethren; in the midst of the assembly I will sing praises to you.'

Hebrews 2:11–12

Herein lies a mystery. That, as we joyfully sing the praises of God, Christ is present in the midst of his people flowing into their minds with the glory and character of God, which releases us from the fear of death (Ezekiel 37:14).

My dreams have lifted me out of the mire of low self-esteem and placed a continual song of praise on my lips and love in my heart as I have experienced life to the full and discovered the joy of a "dream fulfilled"!

Reflective Thinking is written to the Glory of God the Father, God the Son and God the Holy Spirit, and I pray that it will inspire you to pick up the Bible and read it – not as a boring, out-dated book, but as a book full of life, fun, misery, death, destruction, beauty, hope, joy, adultery, forgiveness, murder, intrigue, literature, poetry... all the things that make us human and give reason to start a new life, bringing vision for a brighter future.

Amen.

Chapter One

A Long Walk

On that first Easter Sunday, when the disciples saw the risen Christ, they "clasped his feet, falling prostrate before him" (Matthew 28:9). Our feet are important, for they bear the whole weight of the body: "How beautiful on the mountain are the feet of him who brings good tidings" (Isaiah 52:7), and Jesus' feet must have seemed beautiful to the disciples as they saw him walking up the mount towards them and saying: "Do not be afraid". For three years previously, Jesus walked all around the sea of Galilee proclaiming the kingdom of God, then came the long walk to Golgotha as Jesus walked the way of the Cross to his death. Everyone thought that was the end.

Not so.

Who knows why or how the Spirit of Christ stills walks the globe inspiring the heart, mind and spirit, strengthening people's resolve to walk the way of the cross? Walking through the parables and teachings of Jesus requires the long walk of faith as we learn to put our money where our mouth is, and maybe it will always be so. Therefore, if you want to find out who you really are, as distinct from what you would like to be, keep an eye on where your feet take you!

Prayer

Lord, teach me to take the long road of faith
As I travel through life,
Knowing that you are always with me,
Even to the end of time.
Amen.

Chapter Two

Anxiety

People have become insecure about their future, and it seems that all the advancements of science and technology cannot secure the dream-world hoped for during the 1950s when it was thought that better education, full employment and advances being made in science and technology would cure all our ills. Maybe the very things that have given us a better standard of living have helped to contribute towards some of the anxieties about the unpredictable aspects of the changes and uncertainties we see in society, the political aspirations of nations and climatic change.

Mothers are no longer sure if they should vaccinate their children against measles with the MMR vaccine, fearing their children might develop autism; then there are political questions about what we can do to have a safe society without the threat of terrorism. The London bombings of Thursday 7 July have been a sharp reminder – as well as insecurity in the workplace, street violence and the questioning of medical ethics, a new morality relating to gender issues, justice and peace in the affairs of the world where even politicians are no longer trusted to speak truthfully about security information. Workers are shocked to discover that the systems created by management or government do not support arbitration or reconciliation, and prove too fragile to bear the weight of their hopes.

It awakens within us the fear that the future can no longer be predictable or taken for granted and even brings us to question science, advanced technology or even to doubt the belief systems of the past where God was seen as all-powerful.

Because the present looks gloomy, politicians like to focus our attention on their policies, wanting us to believe that a little hardship in the short term will bring long-term benefits for the future, but no one seems to believe them any more, and people have become anxious.

Anxiety can consume our inner strength and rob us of our God-given potential, which has helped past generations to face their unpredictable future by becoming appreciative of the present.

To help us concentrate on the positive, I turn to Matthew 6:19–33: "Do not be anxious about tomorrow"; the uncertainties of tomorrow can have a crippling effect, turning our attention away from the certainties of the present moment. "Look at the birds of the air... Consider how the lilies grow in the field..." Sometimes it might be healthier to look around us and discover the natural beauty of the earth and the things we take for granted. For example, watching the sunrise, walking in the rain and feeling the wind in our face, these things do not change, but our perception can change as we grow accustomed to the obvious. Therefore we need to "become like little children" (Matthew 18:1–3) once again and rediscover the wonder of seeing the first snowflake, the first flower, bird, flash of lightning, the brightness of the stars, and the wonder of the world! It seems the solution to regain hope lies in looking beyond earthly resources to seek the kingdom of heaven by looking afresh through the eyes of a child?

Prayer

Lord, give me grace to see your kingdom,
Present in the daily routine of life,
And make me see life anew every morning.
Amen.

Chapter Three
Clenched Fist/Open Hand

A clenched fist is usually held up as a symbol of protest or rebellion and when shaken in the direction of another person, becomes the sign of anger, threatening aggression.

In biblical terms it is often seen as a sign of a rebellious nature or hardening of the heart against God: "An evil man seeks only rebellion" (Proverbs 17:11). In our day there are many names for the clenched fist (hooliganism and road rage come to mind immediately). Even fundamentalists, those who hold dogmatic religious or political views, seem to clench their fist and cock a snook at those who hold different values on life.

Whereas the open hand symbolises peace, welcome and friendship; as partakers in Christ, we are asked to offer *Shalom*, peace, to extend the open hand. "Today, if you hear his voice, do not harden your hearts as in the rebellion" (Hebrews 15). To achieve the position of the open hand we need to rediscover the life of prayer, to have access to the spirit of truth that leads us into the realm of forgiveness and salvation.

Do you have a clenched fist or an open hand?

Prayer

Lord, there are times when without knowing what I do,
I clench my fist in silent prayer of protest
When I feel useless at the sight of injustice to the poor,
And cry out "how long, O God?"
During times like this,
Hold me in the palm of your open hand,
And help me realise that
Even in the darkest hour of the night
You surprise us through the babe of Bethlehem.
Help me to open my hands
And lift them up to you in praise and sing:
"Glory be to God on high".
Amen.

Chapter Four

Crown Green Bowling

With the code of crown green bowling it is important to keep your eye on the block and know whether it is sent off from the mat with a "thumb" or "finger" peg and follow the bias of the block. If you keep your eye on the block and use the right bias, you have a good chance of pegging with your wood, in other words, getting close to the block. If you do not keep your eye on the block and send it off with a wrong peg, you are liable to land up in the ditch or go in the wrong direction!

Life, too, has its rules. There is a proper way to live, which has the ring of truth promoting trust and fair play, which is biased in the right direction to help to achieve our goal. If we neglect the rules, we miss the point.

When Thomas enquired the way, Jesus replied: "I am the way, the truth, and the life" (John 14:6).

Prayer

Lord, may I always have my eye on you
And be aware of your presence in all I do.
Amen.

Chapter Five

Discovery

Everyone we encounter in our human relationships helps draw out of us some aspect of our nature and helps to enrich our personality. However, it is in a relationship with God alone that I believe we find out our true identity, it is why prayer has a profound healing effect and is an asset when we are not at ease within ourselves.

Prayer takes our focus from being self-centred to God-centred, taking us on a journey of discovery about who we truly are and where we rightly belong. As we search for meaning we drift into a series of relationships to seek identity, autonomy and freedom. Our search for freedom can bring upon us a feeling of loneliness, because included in our search for freedom we seek to acquire wealth, good living, a happy sex life, and experimentation maybe with drugs, alcohol or casual relationships. Although these seem helpful, even beneficial to our well-being in the short term, once money dries up, friends disappear, and we find we are down on our uppers, we become anxious or depressed thinking we have come to the end of the road.

This is not the end, but the start of discovering our true identity.

If, during this time of grief and disillusionment, we take the courage to sit down and focus on God in prayer, like the prodigal, we begin our journey back home and discover our identity and true worth as a person.

We may also hear the encouraging words of welcome: "This my child was lost, but is found; was dead, but is now alive" (Luke 15:32).

It is a journey we all need to take, one that takes us away from self-centredness into liberation and to be fully known by God as we are known to others, but most of all ourselves.

Prayer

Father God, thank you for being ever watchful
And waiting up for me to return home safely;
Thank you for being compassionate
And understanding my need
To want to be free of parental and other relationships,
Which seemingly restrict my call to be free.
Thank you for being there when my flight for freedom
Becomes my downfall and prison,
For understanding my need to discover myself
And who I am,
And thank you for placing me in your household
As your child once again.
Amen.

Chapter Six

Being a Neighbour

Loving your neighbour as yourself (Galatians 5:14) is not a soft option and is spirit, rather than flesh-facilitated.

When we turn our back on the needs of others and seek self-interest, we devour one another and are consumed by our own desires; the fruit of our labour leads to outbursts of violence, selfish ambition and dissensions.

The process of being a good neighbour requires long-suffering kindness, being faithful and gentleness; these things require self-control. Christ set the pattern of being a neighbour to all people, when he humbled himself (Philippians 2:4) and we are asked to clothe ourselves with that same humility (1 Peter: 5:5).

Looking at humility through the eyes of Christ is not weakness, but takes strength and courage.

When, on selfish grounds, we ask: "Who is my neighbour?" we usually seek birds of a feather and ignore the needs of others outside our circle. But loving our neighbour is a risky business (Luke 10:29). Have the leaders of the recent G8 summit taken enough risks on our behalf to eliminate the debts of the poorer nations and taken enough actions to safeguard our environment?

Prayer

Lord, teach me how to love.
Help me to look over the horizon of self-interest
To the needs of those who live beyond my short
     sightedness,
And strengthen my resolve to recognise the needs of
     others.
Amen.

Chapter Seven

Eternity

We tend to think of eternity as something we enter into after death: a future event. Maybe eternity is not in opposition to time, but the essence of it? Perhaps it is analogous to a coloured spinning top that is rotating at speed, when all the colours blend together to create white; like the spectrum of light, which after passing through a crystal prism makes up the colours of the rainbow.

Maybe if we could spin time fast enough we might enter time past and time future, in time present? We know that all time comes to pass; time waits for no one! We also know that we tend to understand many things in hindsight and our overall understanding of history seems to be tied up with the time past, present and future. It is through that window of events we sometimes catch a glimpse of what it might mean to be human and tell our individual story against a backcloth of events we call family history.

"He has put eternity in their hearts" (Ecclesiastes 3:11) and God who inhabits eternity also has one foot in time (Isaiah 57:15) and God entered time through the Word made flesh (John 1:14). Jesus came to give us a glimpse of eternity by offering us life eternal (John 10:28).

Chapter Eight

Evil

Whenever we see the results of war, natural disaster, people starving and in general criminals making a good living and not being punished, we raise our hands in protest and cry: "How can there be a God of love"?

If God is supposed to be all-powerful, if God is supposed to be good, why do terrible things still happen? It is impossible to reconcile this "trinity", and all religions struggle with this. Faith is unable to solve the problem of evil when it comes down to children being sexually abused, people being murdered, women being raped, and when we are mugged, robbed or treated unjustly.

No words of comfort can ease our pain; and that evil exists cannot be denied. Although there is no satisfactory theological explanation, we have to turn to the cross of Good Friday and say that there is no evil intent in the world that cannot be turned around by God, for the good; "for God so loved the world" (John 3:16).

Prayer

Father, in the midst of evil,
We thank you for the power of your love
Made known to us in the death and resurrection of your
    Son our Lord.
Lead us not into temptation, but deliver us from evil.
Amen.

Chapter Nine

Faith

Faith is a gift that is built into human nature, but is often tucked away into the attics of our minds gathering dust. It is seen as surplus to daily living, but waiting to be taken out and rubbed as a magic lantern when we need help that cannot be found through tried and trusted methods of understanding.

When Abraham was a hundred years old and his wife, Sarah, was ninety, they had to reach into the attics of their minds to find their faith to trust God's promise that Sarah would be with child in her old age. At first it was a laughing matter for Sarah, for her faith had gathered so much dust she had to really rub hard to trust the impossible! So with one foot in the grave and one foot in the maternity ward, she laughed her head off.

So what is faith? "Faith gives substance to our hopes, and makes us certain of realities we do not see" (Hebrews 11:1), and faith is God's laughter, it is laughter built into the name of a child called Isaac (Genesis 21:3).

As long as faith resides in the attics of our minds, it is of little worth and proves nothing, but once replaced into the workshop of the mind, dusted down and rubbed clean; wow! It helps us to achieve the impossible.

Prayer

Lord, help me where faith falls short.
Amen.

Mark 9:24

Chapter Ten

Forgiveness

"I will be merciful to their wicked deeds, and I will remember their sins no more" (Hebrews 8:12).

These are comforting words from the author of Hebrews, and to be forgiven is a wonderful feeling of a friendship being restored.

When we have hurt or upset someone we love, it leaves a bitter taste in our mouth, but when we learn to forgive, and ourselves know we are forgiven, our taste buds flourish, we regain our appetite and life seems sweet once again.

Forgive others and overlook their shortcomings; it helps to restore a relationship.

A forgiving spirit finds ways to overcome the errors we make in life and is of vital importance when little things build up to blight relationships, which frequently happens in marriage, church fellowships or other organisations, where people end up not speaking to one another. Perhaps we should act – before resentment grows – by bringing the situation before God. The more we live in the forgiving light of God, the more we become people who are likely to forgive others. The more our hearts are open to the forgiving love of Christ; the more our relationships will contribute to our own growth and that of others, driving away the destructive forces of guilt, resentment and remorse.

Prayer

Lord, there are many times I have hurt
And upset members of my family, friends and
  neighbours
By not thinking before I speak,
And have used words
Which have not comforted or strengthened our
  relationship.
Give me a forgiving heart,
A tongue that is guided by compassion
And let me be always mindful of your love.
Amen.

Chapter Eleven

Giving

There once was a blind beggar who earned his living playing a tin whistle on the streets of Manchester. One day he heard that Pope John Paul II was visiting Heaton Park and he made his way to the park to sit where the Pope was expected to pass. Right enough there he was on time; with the sound of happy laughter of children following him around the park. Suddenly, there was silence as the Pope stopped to speak to the blind beggar and blessed him; the blind beggar was so pleased that without thinking, he gave the Pope his tin whistle as a gift.

After the Pope had gone he thought to himself, *I have given away my tin whistle, my only source of income, how will I manage?* And as he got up to go back to the city centre, he noticed he could see people as if seeing through a fog. His vision improved till he could see normally, having received his sight, and to his surprise he discovered that the Pope had given him a golden flute in exchange for his tin whistle!

Each person should give as he has decided for himself; there should be no reluctance, no sense of compulsion; God loves a generous giver. And it is in God's power to provide you richly with every good gift.

2 Corinthians 9:7–8

Prayer

Lord, grant me a generous heart,
That I may always give freely according to my means.
Amen.

Chapter Twelve

Grace

What a wonderful concept, grace! Its properties are mysterious and it is a gift that cannot be bought at any price and is above the law (Romans 4:14), freeing us from the burden of sin. Grace is something we can only get as given, it cannot be awarded for work rendered or purchased nor does it come as a birthright. The irritating fact about grace is that you don't have to do anything to deserve it, nothing at all; it is a divine gift (Luke 2:40), and that is why Jesus was full of it (John 1:14). It brings communities into being (Acts 18:27), and makes us what we are (1 Corinthians 15:10).

With grace, we are not afraid and nothing can separate us; with it, we are reassured of the continuing presence of Jesus. It is beyond our understanding. With it, the universe was created and is continually sustained by its love.

Jesus is God's grace given out for us.

There is only one snag. Like any other gift, you have to open your hands to reach out and receive it!

Prayer

Let the healing grace of your love, O Lord,
So transform me that I play my part in transforming
   your world.
Amen.

Chapter Thirteen

Boxing Clever

One thing I have learnt from boxing is to size up the opposition and to keep out of the corner. It is best to keep to the centre of the ring and leave your options open, moving to the left or the right depending on the opponent's stance. If you face an orthodox boxer, one who leads with the left hand, move to your right; if a southpaw who leads with the right, then move to your left.

Likewise, on life's journey, we should use discernment in all situations and avoid being trapped with our backs against the wall leaving no room to manoeuvre. It is best to box clever, feeling your way, ducking and diving and protecting the body and chin to survive in life rather than being knocked out.

Learning the art of discussion and persuasion takes more skill and allows us to live to fight another day (Genesis 18:16–33).

Prayer

Lord, be with me when I am trapped in the corner
With my back on the ropes.
Help me to keep up my guard, and protect myself
   from the blows;
Strengthen my legs that they do not buckle under
   the onslaught,
And clear my head.
Put a spring in my toes
That I may dance back to the centre of the ring
To continue the fight.
Amen.

Chapter Fourteen

Law of the Jungle

The law of the jungle seems to work well in the wilds, where animals have learnt to adapt to the law of survival, a kind of "kill or be killed" code; where one animal will wait in hiding to ambush another that is vulnerable, or attack the weak and lame who become easy prey.

It may also hold sway in the absence of a "civilised" humanitarian society, in a world that lacks law and order; where a person or persons may sit lurking in a secret place with eyes fixed on unsuspecting victims, or draw them into a trap, as a lion in its den, to oppress or murder the helpless.

In an uncivilised society, the strong may be able to defend themselves, but the poor, weak, and helpless have to cry out to God.

> Their mouths are filled with cursing and deceit and oppression; under their tongues are mischief and iniquity. They sit in ambush in the villages; in hiding places they murder the innocent. Their eyes stealthily watch for the helpless; they lurk in secret like a lion in its covert; they lurk that they may seize the poor; they seize the poor and drag them off in their net. They stoop, they crouch, and the helpless fall by their might. They think in their heart, "God has forgotten, he has hidden his face, he will never see it."
>
> Psalms 10:7–11

Our hope rests in God: God hears the cry of the poor and will "do justice to the fatherless and the oppressed, that the man of the earth may oppress no more" (Psalms 10:18).

Prayer

Lord, help me to be open and honest in my dealings
    with others
And not to be afraid of giving others a fair chance;
To present their side of the story,
Even if it means being exposed to ridicule or being
    cheated,
And may I always be mindful of the poor.
Amen.

Chapter Fifteen

Leadership

True leadership involves service, humility and being transparent as one learns to be both student and teacher.

Start by going to the people and live among them as one, sharing your gifts of bread and learning from them how to make wine for a celebration banquet. Commence with all that is true within a community and affirms peace and unity, use them as the foundation stone to build a new society and when the task is accomplished; walk away and release the reins of authority by encouraging inexperienced leaders to recognise their gifts. When that is done, leave quietly so the people can exclaim: "Look what we have done by ourselves!"

Jesus arose from supper and laid aside his garments, took a towel and girded himself. After that, he poured water into a basin and began to wash the disciples' feet, and to wipe them with the towel with which he was girded.

Then he said: "If I your lord and teacher, have washed your feet, you also ought to wash one another's feet'. I have set you an example."

John 13:5–15

Prayer

Lord, whenever I am placed in a position of
   authority or leadership,
Help me to remember those who have elected me,
And to serve humbly, seeking no other reward,
But doing my duty joyfully.
Amen.

Chapter Sixteen

Letting Go

"Letting go" is one of the most difficult emotions we experience in life. From the time of our conception to the time of death we seem to face a series of letting go. We have to let go of the womb, mother's breast and sucking our thumbs, nursery, infants, secondary or grammar schools, college or university; letting go youth, family, work, and those we love.

And as Shakespeare put it in *As You Like It*:"Last scene of all, / That ends this strange eventful history, / Is...Sans teeth, sans eyes, sans taste, sans everything."

It seems like all our series of letting go is like "little deaths and new beginnings".

When we take courage and let go, we grow and discover new territory and ways of doing things, giving a wider horizon to life; when we fail to let go, we do not grow and mature to be independent adults. Often the most difficult time of letting go comes when we lose a loved one and good friend; then we tend to cling on and freeze our life, turning our back to new opportunities.

"Whoever seeks to save his life will lose it; and whoever loses it will save it, and live" (Luke 17:33).

Prayer

Lord, help me to discern the important things in life from
   the trivial,
That I do not fill the attic of my mind,
Keeping hold of the past, just in case I need it.
Give me the grace to let go all that seems to comfort me
And prevents me from reaching out to new opportunities
That, dying to the old, I might find new life.
Amen.

Chapter Seventeen

Loneliness

In one way or another we all carry a deep wound of loneliness, and most of us try to avoid being alone and tend to cover it up by being overactive in a thousand and one ways. Or we try to deal with loneliness by joining clubs, community life and other social activities believing they will help to alleviate being in the doldrums.

While we are young and full of energy and bright ideas we find means and ways to hide our disappointment at being alone, or flee the present by projecting into the future, thinking "it will all work out in the end and things might be better tomorrow".

But tomorrow never seems to come and by the time we are forty-something, the future seems to have missed us and we end up feeling depressed, especially since we carry all the guilt and apathy of the past, which now becomes a burden for us to carry on our shoulders. We start to realise that maybe this wound of loneliness is inherent in human nature and that we have to learn to deal with it rather than flee from it.

Faith is the healing balm that comes to our aid, and we discover that we are loved by God just as we are, and that our loneliness is to do with our human spirit, which needs the breath of God's Spirit to heal the centre of our wound. The Spirit of God then walks beside our spirit guiding, leading and directing us towards maturity and wisdom; leading us through the "dark night" of our soul. We enter into a world of confusion where we encounter our loneliness, and the Spirit of God infuses with our spirit uniting it with God and the wound of loneliness is healed. We are reconciled with our true self, able to love ourself, to no longer feel alone, and to discover love for others with the new found love of God. In that sense, we are born again.

"What man of you, having a hundred sheep, if he loses one of them, does not leave the ninety-nine in the wilderness, and go after the one which is lost, until he finds it?" (Luke 15:4)

Prayer

Lord, there are times I feel alone
And lost in a world of my own
And it seems that no one cares,
But when I read the parables your Son told
To help teach us that you are always there, looking
    out for us,
I know that I will be found
And that you will carry me on the shoulder of your
    love
And restore me back to life,
To live in community with others once again.
Amen.

Chapter Eighteen

Mystery

Two things are necessary to know the mystery of God:

One is to see the world through revelation by the Holy Spirit, and the second is a response from the heart.

There are three ways of knowing:

The first is through the eye, which has not seen, the ear, which has not heard,

The second through the Spirit who comes from God;

And the third is found in the depth of our being.

> Eye has not seen, nor ear heard, nor have entered into the heart of man,
> The things which God has prepared for those who love Him.

> 1 Corinthians 2:9

But God has revealed them to us through His Spirit. For the Spirit searches all things, yes, and the deep things of God.

Now we have received, not the spirit of the world, but the Spirit who is from God, that we might know the things that have been freely given to us by God. These things we also speak, not in words, which man's wisdom teaches but which the Holy Spirit teaches, comparing spiritual things with spiritual.

But the natural man does not receive the things of the Spirit of God, for they are foolishness to him; nor can he know them, because they are spiritually discerned. But he who is spiritual judges all things; yet no one rightly judges him himself. For "who has known the mind of the Lord that he may instruct Him?" But we have the mind of Christ.

Prayer

Lord, grant me the eyes of faith
That I may see your works in all creation,
Visible and invisible.
Amen.

Chapter Nineteen

No Hiding Place

It seems that nothing in creation can escape the eyes of God, for all things are open to his gaze; it can be deeply disturbing that God can invade our privacy, leaving us feeling helpless.

Yet God reaches out to us in the person of his Son, who is able to sympathise with our weakness and helps us to build a bridge between God and humanity. The crucified Christ is the very presence of God's grace in time of need.

Having gone through temptation, sorrow, pain, and dejection by his suffering on the cross, Jesus provides a path to approach God with confidence knowing that we are forgiven; in as much as God's grace is sufficient.

> The word of God is alive and active. It cuts more keenly than any two-edged sword, piercing as far as the place where life and spirit, joints and marrow, divide. It sifts the purpose of the heart.

Hebrews 14:12

Prayer

Lord, please do not let me out of your sight,
Find me when I am lost,
And reassure me of your continuing presence.
Amen.

Chapter Twenty

On Prayer

As oil to a machine
Prayer is to the soul.

Prayer is first and foremost about a relationship between God and us, and forms the basis of all our other relationships, making it the place where we discover our true identity. As machinery needs oil, prayer is anointing oil, lubricating the soul to form a meaningful relationship with God. Unfortunately, modern culture has distanced itself from such an important relationship, presenting us with an alternative, that of self-discovery; creating the cult of individualism, persuading us to believe that true happiness is to be found by delving into the shadows of our mind and human relationships, enabling us to satisfy our wanton desires. This process is supposed to free a person to be their true self, but it seems to be a short-term affair as Jesus demonstrates in the parable of the prodigal son (Luke 15).

Therefore, scripture teaches us that we are beings in relationship to God and to discover our true identity as His sons and daughters; that we are all sisters and brothers at heart, through this primary relationship.

It is also true to say that on the pure human level, the foundational relationship we have in common is through our "primary care-givers". Although these may be our parents, it could be anyone who is our initial carer and it is they who help lay the foundations of personality through nurture. But families and carers alike are not perfect, and consequently we all grow up with certain quirks. Where families are dysfunctional, they fail to do the basic job they are meant to do and they can have a crippling effect on a person's well-being.

This is where the importance of prayer and its relationship to God comes as welcome news. God's call of love enables us to "kick start" our life, turn it around; He forgives our past failures and gives us permission and encouragement to rediscover our true selves. Because we are beings in relationship to others, we tend to be different things to different people and this can confuse our understanding of what we are meant to be. By trying to please all people, we usually end up being false to ourselves and in this way we are all dysfunctional personalities in one way or another. Consequently, all other decisions we make in life fall short of the ideals we hold and we are left feeling guilty, anxious and not totally at ease with life.

Through the parable of the prodigal son, Jesus gives us an insight into someone making a journey of discovery about their true identity and returning to their home roots.

The disciples saw Jesus as a son who had a special relationship with God through the way he prayed, and they also wanted to learn how to communicate to God as Father, and so they asked: "Lord, teach us how to pray" (Luke 11:1–4).

We all need role models in life. When I was learning to box and because I was small, Jimmy Wild, a flyweight and world champion became my hero and inspiration. Whenever we see someone who excels in the field of their profession, be it in sport, music or drama, they make things look easy and graceful by their movement. What we fail to see straightaway is the discipline and long hours of practice it takes to reach the stage where mind, body and spirit flow in one graceful movement. Prayer is no different. Prayer does not just happen, as if out of the blue! Like any other aspect of life, first of all, we need to desire what we truly want.

"As the deer pants for water brooks, so pants my soul for you, O God" (Psalms 42:1).

Prayer is about relationship.

A way to get to know a person is to start a conversation, and during our conversation, as we exchange information we develop a relationship. Prayer is like that and although at first it may seem as if you are talking to yourself, maybe you will discover another voice echoing within bringing peace and stillness.

As St Augustine once said, "Our hearts are restless till they find their rest in thee".

Like all relationships we form in life, we need to have a yearning to discover something about the people who attract our attention; the heart needs to be stirred as our hands reach out to be introduced to the person we long to meet. In the case of prayer, the heart needs to long for God: "My soul thirsts for God, for the living God" (Psalms 42:2). Prayer is a relationship of sending and receiving the longings and depth of our being. When mind, body and spirit are entwined and embraced by prayer we are transformed and become more human and this is translated in the way we interact with our neighbour and the environment, for in Christ we become a new creation (2 Corinthians 5:17). Together with others who follow the way, we become a single body (1 Corinthians 12:12) and have an impact on the community in which we dwell.

The prayer Jesus taught us, *Our Father*, is the basis of our relationship with God and does not rest on our lips, but dwells deep within the heart. This relationship, like all meaningful relationships, has to be cultivated and developed by lifelong experience of give and take and requires humility, patience, forgiveness, love, kindness – the attributes which help shape character to bring out the best in human nature; where being and doing become one action as expressed in the sacrificial act of God's love displayed by Christ on Good Friday.

If we want to learn to play an instrument we need to learn the theory of music; know more about the instrument we have a longing to play; find someone who can teach us and practice, practice, practice till the instrument, music and the self become the tune. It is the same with prayer: it takes practice, practice, practice.

Prayer is an activity of mind, body and spirit and therefore we have to be comfortable and require a place where we are at ease and the body feels restful where we can "be still and know God" (Psalms 46:10), and a useful formula to adopt is ACTS: Adoration, Confession, Thanksgiving and Supplication. It has been a well-used and useful method of entering into prayers for many years. Practice this daily – as if you were learning to read music and play an instrument – until it becomes part of your every movement and you will automatically join in the rhythm of prayer and experience healing in mind, body and spirit. It is helpful to find a quiet spot and open your Bible to the prayers of the psalmists.

> Let my cry come before you, O Lord;
> Give me understanding according to your word.
> Let my supplication come before you,
> Deliver me according to your word.

> Psalms 119:169–170

Adoration

When we first sit down in silence we may experience a lot of noise from within: the echoes of the mind and the various demands upon our time, each vying for attention. Therefore, it takes time before we enter the deep place of prayer.

We have to be patient and wait till the confusion within our mind settles and we begin to relax in our own company, then a miracle seems to take place as we relax into God's pervading presence into that world we call prayer!

It is from that place we listen as God speaks through the silence. We enter into the presence of God in which our soul feels free.

Begin by silent adoration as you rest in the presence of God.

The most beautiful and heartfelt cries of prayer are written in the Psalms, keep them beside you, reflect and be still. "Great is the Lord; and greatly to be praised" (Psalms 48:1).

Use your imagination let your thoughts flow freely, do not be afraid to let go and let God be near you, surrounding you, holding you in his loving arms.

> Father God, I love you and long to see your face,
> My heart longs for you and my flesh to hold you,
> Because you are kind and loving my lips praise you
> And my hands reach up to the sky.

When we are in the presence of someone whom we look up to and respect, we are humbled and turn to reflect on things that we have not completed, or have undertaken half-heartedly and with the psalmist can cry out: "Be merciful to me, O God, be merciful to me! For my soul trusts you" (Psalms 57:1).

Confession

The word "confession" is often seen unfavourably and gets a bad press in modern society; maybe a better word is "acknowledgment"? When we acknowledge we have faults then we have started the process to turn things around and make amends.

"Have mercy upon me, O God, according to your loving kindness" (Psalms 51:1).

When we are humble enough to admit our faults it has a freeing effect on the mind and relaxes the body, and the spirit within feels at ease, for "God is our refuge and strength, a very present help in trouble. Therefore we will not fear" (Psalms 46:1).

Fear has a paralysing effect and holds us prisoners, preventing us from achieving what we are capable of. When we have acknowledged our faults and been forgiven, then we are restored once more. Knowing that God is with us and accepts us as we are, we can clap our hands and rejoice, shout to God with a new voice of praise and sing "joyfully to the Rock of our salvation. Let us shout joyfully to Him with psalms" (Psalms 95:1–2).

Thanksgiving

When we are forgiven, we feel loved, and like Daniel can cry:

> I thank you and praise you, O God of my fathers; you have given me wisdom and might, and have made known to me what we asked of you
>
> Daniel 2:23

Or, like the psalmist:

I will bless the Lord who has given me counsel and instructs me; therefore my heart is glad and my glory rejoices; my flesh also will rest in hope; and in your presence is the fullness of joy

Psalms 16:7–11

The psalms are beautiful prayers of the people of God and there are psalms for every occasion and feeling our human nature can express, be it in the doldrums or gliding like a bird in the sky.

Supplication

When we find ourselves in the presence of God, having given him his true worth by worshipping and adoring him; we discover how far we fall short of fulfilling our potential to be human and once again feel loved and restored to become sons and daughters of the living God and learn the depth of the prayer Jesus taught (the *Our Father*), and start to pray for the needs of others in the community and world. Because the soul is free we can appreciate the words of St Augustine: "Love God, and do whatever you please", because the soul that loves God loves all his creation and will help care for it. Being thankful to God for what he has done for us leads us to look outward to the needs and concerns of others and pray for them.

And finally,

Rejoice in the Lord always. Again I will say, rejoice! Be anxious for nothing, but in everything by prayer and supplication, with thanksgiving, let your requests be made known to God; and the peace of God, which surpasses all understanding, will guard your hearts and minds through Christ Jesus.

Philippians 4:4–7

Now that you have learnt to pray, just practice, practice, practice and keep praying and singing from your heart!

Chapter Twenty-one

Our Streets Through the Eyes of the Poor

Most of us live within a family or social context where goals are set, ambition fostered, luxuries hoped for, holidays planned and life seems reasonably comfortable.

When we view our streets from the lens of respectability, conformity, safety and contentment we tend to see our streets as areas where we go shopping for food, clothing, furniture, and luxury items and where we look for cheap holidays through the window of travel agents. When we are privileged to be in such a position, our streets may also be seen as threatening places as we become aware of potential muggings, robberies, drunkenness and violence. Viewing the streets through the eyes of the poor, things look different.

By the poor, I do not mean the unwaged who live on the dole or government and council handouts to give them a standard living wage with subsidies for holidays and luxury items, but those who live on our streets by choice or necessity. These are the ones who fall outside the benefits system, National Health Service, housing and other benefits; who rely on charitable organisations for a night's shelter, food, clothing and general care with the aim of rehabilitation into the system of things. These are the marginalized within our society where the street is their home; the very ones who become vulnerable to the muggings, robberies, drunkenness and violence on our street. Viewing the streets through the eyes of the marginalized poor, it is society – the people who live in homes, the ones who have the good life, the ones advertisers entice to be "with it", "be cool", the respectable ones – that look threatening.

Whereas we look around for the best shops to do our shopping, the poor who live on our streets have to draw a different kind of map for the locality in which they dwell.

The first and most important requirement is: "Where are the public toilets?" and then, "Where do the 'soup runs' take place?" and "Where are the clothing distribution points situated?" so that they have the chance of a change of attire. They have to find the place where it is possible to have a wash down, maybe get some sort of physical check-up and some respite for a night's shelter.

These are provided by charitable organisations, both Christian and humanitarian; sometimes assisted by government and local councils who do not generally cater for the poor.

To the street dwellers, Christmas and the organisation, Shelter, are synonymous, it is the one time their plight is made public. Food, shelter and clothing are made available in church halls, disused public buildings. They are given special attention with helpers rallying around offering a listening ear, a cigarette and showing that elements of society really do care.

Why can't it be Christmas every day?

> He who oppresses the poor reproaches his Maker,
> But he who honours Him has mercy on the needy.

Proverbs 14:31

Chapter Twenty-two

Peace

Jesus brings *Shalom*, a peace which incorporates wholeness and harmony on every level of life, the balm of our salvation. It is a peace that flows through experiencing forgiveness, drawing our attention to the hurt that lurks within us, and the harm we do to others because we are wounded; helping us to recognise our needs and humbly to seek forgiveness and be prepared to say we are sorry. Then the peace of God, which is beyond our understanding, drives away fear and anxiety. In one way or another we are all damaged goods: damaged through relationships, left vulnerable and bewildered, traumatised and left feeling deeply hurt in some aspects of our life journey. Be it through premature separation from a parent, through divorce, redundancy, illness, abuse (physical or sexual), failure to achieve, resulting in fear, guilt and shame. Many of these bad memories are pushed below and surface as aggression, mental illness, resentment, distrust and so on, distorting our view of the world and making us ignorant to the knowledge that life could be lived differently. Into this distorted and dark world of our soul, Jesus brings peace. *Shalom*.

"Peace I leave you: it is my peace I give you" (John 20:19–23).

Prayer

> Lord, come into my life
> And remove all that harms me
> And bring me your peace.
> Amen.

Prayers from a Loving Heart

Lord, please do not take Your Holy Spirit away from me.
Loving God, take my body, mind and spirit,
Cleanse me of my faults, and redeem my soul
Making me Yours alone.
Amen.

My dear Jesus, guide me by Your perpetual light.
Fill me with Your Holy Spirit,
Till my heart is full of love.
Amen.

Father, in Thy image we are created;
Son of the Father, in thy light we bathe;
Holy Spirit, advocate and guide,
Lead us to worship Thee, three in one and one in three.
In perfect unity; Father, Son and Holy Spirit.
Amen.

Lord, teach me how to pray.
Apprentice me in Your school of love
So I may love and serve You with all my heart.
Amen.

Heavenly Father, here I am.
Because You love me, I can come to You.
Because You are merciful, I am made worthy.
Because of You, I am.
Amen.

Merciful Lord, take away from me
All that distorts my relationship with others;
Take away from me my heart of stone,
And give me a heart of flesh,
A heart to love and adore You,
That following in Your footsteps
I may find it in my heart to forgive
And love others as You forgive and love me.
Amen.

Lord, thank you for making me human;
For giving me mind, body and spirit;
For giving me the gift of sight, taste, touch, smell
And the ability to hear Your word in creation.
When things go wrong and I misuse or abuse Your gifts
For selfish reasons or for my own advantage,
Forgive me,
And by Your grace draw me to Your bosom
And let me rest in Your arms.
Amen.

Lord, in the silence of this moment
As I thank you for the power of speech,
Help me to listen rather than talk,
To be open to the prompting of Your guiding Spirit
That I may discover a new way of being me,
Free from fear and guilt,
From self-pity or doubt, to be a new creation
And sing like the birds at dawn
To welcome in a new day.
Amen.

Sometimes, I wish I did not know of love,
So I may escape its demands.
But having tasted its nectar,
I do willingly accept its agony.
Amen.

Lord, there are times when I long to be rich and win the
    lottery,
To have enough money to buy the comforts of life
And enjoy the gifts of the earth.
Lord, help me to have enough to satisfy my needs,
That I may sit loosely on wealth
And not let it come between Your love
And the gift of eternal life You bring.
Amen.

Father, we thank you for giving us the will to choose
Whether we take what is due and leave home
And learn the ways of the world,
Or stay at home and await our rewards.
Give us courage and wisdom
To learn from experiences of the ups and downs of life.
Amen.

Father God, when You created us in Your image,
You created us male and female.
But sometimes the male and female gender is placed in the
    wrong body
And causes perplexity and heated debate in Your Church;
And much suffering to the persons involved.
When we pray to seek Your will,
How is that we get muddled messages?
If Your Son died to save the world,
Doesn't it mean all of us, no matter what our condition?
And if so, why the division and debate in the church?
Help us dear Lord, to be tolerant of others,
Understanding that "there but for the grace of God".
Amen.

Slow me down, Lord.
Ease the pounding of my heart by the quieting of my mind.
Teach me the art of slowing down.
To look at a flower,
To chat to a friend,
To rest on Your yoke;
And help me to look into the branches of the towering oak
And know that it grew great and strong
Because it grew slowly and well.
Amen.

Lord, although You said, "the poor will always be among us",
You did not say that they would multiply
As we continue to ignore their needs,
Nor that Your Church would be more interested in
    internal concerns
Of making women bishops and questioning human sexuality;
And that the richer nations would be more concerned
With the wealth of their own people.
Lord, give us eyes to see You in the poor and disadvantaged
And to seek justice on their behalf.
Amen.

Lord, not our gifts alone but our lives also we offer up to You.
Accept both our gifts and us in Your service,
And use them to Your praise and glory.
Amen.

Lord, we bring before You the Church
In all its richness and all its needs,
In all its diversity and division;
Praying that You will give us fresh understanding
Of what it means to be Your people;
May all of us in our various ministries,
Both lay and ordained,
Celebrate Your presence among us,
Filling us with new life and hope.
Amen.

May the love of God the Father hold and embrace you,
May the love of God the Son surround and look over you,
May the love of God the Holy Spirit dwell in you,
And the blessing of God Almighty, Father, Son and Holy
Spirit;
Hold you in the palm of His left hand
And place His right hand over your head to protect you
Now and always.
Amen.

Lord, walk beside me as I journey on the road of life,
Open my eyes to Your truth
And reveal Yourself as the risen Lord
Whenever I share a meal with others in the breaking of
bread.
Equip, inspire and encourage me to understand
That I am Your ambassador
Who proclaims the good news of Your resurrection
And the eternal life it brings.
Amen.

Living God, all You have created is good.
Sharpen my conscience to the wonder, joy, and the beauty
of the earth.
Guide me in the way of truth;
Help me to realign all the values on which I make decisions
That I may know that You are the Way, the Truth and the
Life,
And live my life as a living sacrifice to the glory of Your name.
Amen.

Jesus, my brother and friend,
Your presence is my continual help when all else fails
During those Gethsemane moments in life when, all alone
   in the middle of the night,
I cry to have the cup of suffering taken out of my hands.
During the dark night of anguish when all seems lost;
There You are in the deep, deep of my being
Helping me to say; nevertheless,
"Father, into Your hands I commit my spirit"[1]
And somehow the clouds disappear;
I see a new day with hope on the horizon,
A new place to land, and gain respite from the storm.
Amen.

Lord of Life, we pray for Your Church, militant on earth,
That she may proclaim with boldness Your risen life;
Refresh and breathe into us the breath of Your Holy Spirit,
That, renewed, purified and kindled by Your flame of love,
We may broadcast Your glorious resurrected life to the world.

Lord of life, we pray that the streets
Of our towns and cities
May be safe places to walk;
May our homes be places of peace, joy and hope,
And we pray that in the everyday situations we face in life,
You will be there beside us,
Guiding us to seek Your will in all we do and say.

God of glory, may Your light so shine on Your Church
That she may know Your presence and gift-bearing Spirit,
To serve the communities in which we live;
Bless the various ministries in Your church
And help us offer our souls and bodies to be a living sacrifice,
That we may be seen to be Your servant church serving in
   the world.

---

[1] Luke 23: 46

God of glory, with Your special affection for the outcasts
and marginalized,
The weak and vulnerable, and all who suffer;
We bring before You those known to us who are sick or in
pain:
Stretch out Your hand and touch them
As we pray that they may feel Your glory.
Bring them health in mind, body and spirit.

God of glory, we pray that our homes,
Schools, shops, offices, factories and places of leisure
Will be places where Your glory is experienced in the
ordinary things
And everyday routines of life.

Come, Holy Spirit,
Refresh the earth with Your breath of life
And heal all nations
And give to all in authority the spirit of truth, justice and
compassion,
That the world may become
A place of equal opportunity for all people,
And that the debts of poorer nations
May be erased by the richer nations of the West.

Father God, we bring before You the needs of the Church,
Praying that You will inspire all those who preach the good
news,
We pray for those who teach in our theological colleges
and church schools,
For all who minister in word or sacrament,
And for Your faithful people,
That together we will work and pray for Christian unity
throughout the world.

Father God, we bring before You
The problems of our age and diverse culture,
Praying that all nations will work to create communities of
    mutual trust
And be committed to just trading,
Equal sharing of world resources
And looking after the environment
That future generations may also appreciate the beauty
And wonder of Your creation.

Father God, Son and Holy Spirit, mystery of love and
    unity,
We lift up to You in prayer
All people who have died a natural death
Or have died through war, terrorism or violence
And have not been prepared to face You in death;
We pray for the forgiveness of sin and life everlasting
And that they rest in peace.
We also pray for the recently departed within this
    community, especially...

Chapter Twenty-three

Preparation

On the whole, we tend to neglect the most important function of life: its preparation. Can we imagine sitting down to a meal without first of all collecting the ingredients and preparing them to be cooked? Or building a house without first preparing the ground for the foundations? When Kelly Holmes won her two Olympic Gold Medals, she made it look so easy, but it took years of preparation to help her to achieve her ambition.

If we do not take the same care to prepare for the most important thing in life, our very soul, then it will be our downfall. (Matthew: 25:1–13)

Prayer

Lord, help me to prepare for all I do in life
And not be foolish and forgetful,
Like the five girls, who forgot to buy oil for their lamps.
Amen.

Chapter Twenty-four

Prodigal

In one way or another we are prodigal and we wander off before we are ready to face the world to do our own thing, although that can turn out to be positive; for through our experiences and encounters with other human beings we can start to discover who we truly are. Leaving home and family for the first time can be risky, leading us to a position where we feel as though we have lost the plot, finding ourselves at the bottom of the pile.

But that may not be as bad as it sounds!

For it is from that position we can take stock, look up, and discover our true heritage.

Taking courage to return to our beginnings and being prepared to say "sorry" can be the start of something new.

"For this son of mine was dead and has come back to life; he was lost and is found" (Luke 15:24).

Prayer

Lord, there are many times
When I have felt like taking what is mine and
    leaving home,
During these times of discontent,
Help me to realise that the true treasure resides in
    the heart.
Amen.

Chapter Twenty-five

Relationships

Relationships are part of everyday affairs and take up an enormous amount of time and energy; they are the means through which our love for one another is tested and the reality of our faith exposed.

"If anyone says, 'I love God', yet hates his brother or sister, he or she is a liar" (1 John 4:19–20).

What is our attitude towards parents, husband, wife, relatives, friends, colleagues, casual acquaintances or a stranger? And what are we like when it comes to forgiving or accepting forgiveness; are we quick to condemn or judge others who are different, be it race or culture; and do we allow others to express their opinions without despising them? Once we begin to examine our attitudes and see what we look at through the lens of God we may see things in a new light.

> Since we have been justified through faith, we have peace with God through our Lord Jesus Christ, through whom we have gained access by faith into this grace in which we now stand.
>
> Romans 5:1–2

When we learn to love our neighbour as we have been loved by the grace of God, we become agents of God's healing in the world and having been reconciled to God, become reconciled to one another.

Prayer

"Teach me, O Lord, the way of Your statutes.
And I shall keep it to the end.
Give me understanding,
And I shall keep Your law;
Indeed, I shall observe it with my whole heart.
Make me walk in the path of Your commandments,
For I delight in it."

Psalms 119:33–35

Chapter Twenty-six

Roots

Lord, there are parts of me, which lie hidden deep beneath the surface of my consciousness, and seem harmless while hidden out of sight, but like the roots of a tree when they are exposed, look all gnarled and entwined.

When these strange shapes arise from below the surface of my mind they frighten me, as I learn there is more to me than I first thought, and I am no longer sure of this other me? When this occurs, how I long to cut myself free of this tangled mess and get rid of those messy knots; thinking my life would be better off without them. But, Lord You teach me that these shapes of confusion need healing and are a source of new life, energy and potential love; that I must first try to love and keep in touch with the other me, before I can truly love another person and be free.

Jesus said to his disciples: "Love one another even as I have loved you." (John 13:34)

Prayer

Lord, help me to be unafraid
And to accept myself for who I am,
For if I cut away these strange shapes,
Which make me feel uneasy;
The very sap that gives me food and strength to grow;
Then like a tree severed from its roots,
I will surely die!
Teach me, Lord, to love as you love me.
Amen.

Chapter Twenty-seven

Sexual Union

Making love is one of the most beautiful experiences, and we should be thankful that we have been created in the image of God (Genesis 1:27), and need to praise Him for fashioning us in his likeness. If God is love, then love is a beautiful and wonderful thing and all aspects of love, sacrificial or physical, should be celebrated within the joy of a covenanted relationship, be it marriage or a deep commitment between two people. God has given us many gifts including imagination, intellect and passion. When we use our bodies with care and respect, and in a trusting relationship share that God-given love with another, we share the most beautiful gift of all: our very self. This moment of mutual joy should be seen as a sacrament; an outward sign of two bodies entwined making love, while sharing an inward grace as blessings are bestowed on one another. Like all sacraments, this is God-given and should be taken seriously and not selfishly, for it is something special between two people who care deeply about each other and by sharing this God-given gift, get to know the depth of their being.

> How beautiful are your feet in sandals,
> O prince's daughter!
> The curves of your thighs are like jewels...
>
> Your navel is a rounded goblet...
> Your waist is a heap of wheat
> Set about with lilies,
> Your two breasts are like two fawns...
> Your neck is like an ivory tower.

Song of Songs 7

Prayer

God, our Creator,
We thank you for forming us in your own image
And giving us the ability to form a covenant
  relationship
Through marriage and deep friendship.
We thank you for the beauty and wonder of sexual
  union,
When flesh is entwined with flesh,
And the joy when two hearts beating the rhythm of
  love,
Move in unison from a slow waltz to a rock and
  roll,
Then after the juice of love has flowed,
Two contented lovers can sleep in peaceful
  embrace.
Amen.

Chapter Twenty-eight
Silence

Coming to terms with silence is an important part of gaining self-knowledge and it offers space to be still and listen to God in the echoes of the mind. It helps build up inner resources, which brings healing of the memories and wholeness of body, mind and spirit. We live in a culture which has almost outlawed silence and stillness; therefore, we need to create oases in which inner silence can be cultivated.

Silence also offers space for self-counselling, listening to your inner voice for guidance and understanding the emotional needs of the deep within you. It is a way of entering into the loving silence of God who as the Holy Spirit, the Counsellor, is waiting there to heal you and where the light of Christ, shining in the dark soul helps you to discover the truth about yourself, removing the mask which prevents you from being free. Sometimes, like Samuel it may take an older person to direct you to listen to the voice within, which can lead towards growth and change.

"Speak, Lord, for your servant is listening" (Samuel 3:9).

Prayer

Lord, be in my mind
And in my understanding.
Amen.

Chapter Twenty-nine

Springtime of Faith

Someone speaks a word and a thought is planted in the mind and we go about our business as usual. Life goes on around us and through our daily communication with others we gradually develop a personality and habits that become our own. Just like a plant growing in the ground, we take on our own shape, and learn to weather the wind, rain, sunshine and storm. Then unexpectedly we notice some change has taken place; just like springtime bursting out, and all of a sudden we see the trees and shrubs in full bloom! The candles on the horse chestnut and the may blossom, the cowslips and the honeysuckle in fresh bloom. We notice that springtime has arrived!

Of course things don't just happen overnight, interactions are going on mysteriously, and growth is progressively taking place beneath the ground, then suddenly there comes a moment when we recognise the full breathtaking beauty of nature as she explodes into life.

I believe something like that takes place the first time the reality of God breaks through in our life; it may be through something we experience through reading a book, the birth of a new child, the death of a loved one, a marriage, a new romance, an encounter with a friend or a stranger. These moments of disclosure may produce a special meaning in our relationship with God and help strengthen our bond of relationship with loved ones.

For Christians, worship, prayer and the reading of scripture may be times when we experience an awareness of the living Christ, and we feel special; then daily living takes on new meaning and we discover the ongoing power of love, knowing that God is gracious and we are being reconciled to him through the sacrificial love of Christ. Suddenly we see the wonder of it all a "Eureka moment", the springtime of our life! And we respond with Alleluia!

Jesus said:

> A man scatters seed on the land; he goes to bed at night and gets up in the morning, and the seed sprouts and grows – how, he does not know. The ground produces a crop by itself, first the blade, then the ear, then full-grown corn in the ear; but as soon as the crop is ripe, he plies the sickle, because harvest-time has come.

Mark 4:26–29

Chapter Thirty

Suffering

As an old wives' tale has it: "only the good die young". Suffering is a thorn in the side of religion, a pain in the tooth that won't go away, and at best an unexplainable mystery, which lies in the hands of God. Take Job, for example. Everyone will agree he is a good man minding his own business, and, as they say, hurting no one; yet his cattle are stolen, sheep and servants burned to death, the wind blows down his house while his children are still in it, with none left alive to tell the tale. Now that is suffering; and all he can say is: "the Lord gave and the Lord has taken away, blessed be the name of the Lord". Even after he comes down with boils and his wife, fed up with it all, demands that he curse at God for his bad luck, he manages to bite his tongue. It is only after his friends come along to console him without success that he curses the day he was born and feeling sorry for himself, asks some awkward questions.

It is often said: "If God is all that he is cracked up to be, why do innocent people die, why is there disease, war, famine, natural disaster, drought; why suffering?" Although Job's friends produce a lot of plausible theological reflections, God remains silent on the matter, but he does blast out by asking who does Job think he is anyway? And the words flow like music: "From whose womb comes the ice? And the frost of heaven, who gives it birth? Can you bind the cluster of the Pleiades? Do you know the ordinances of the heavens? Who has given understanding to the heart?"

Job gets a real blasting, but maybe God doesn't give an explanation because it would be impossible to understand and take in the extent of the Divine economy and wisdom of creation. Job doesn't get the answer to suffering, but what he sees through his dialogue is the face of God, and he is humbled into repenting; after which he is blessed with twice as much as he had before. Patient suffering without cursing receives its own reward.

Prayer

Read the Book of Job then make up your own prayer according to your circumstances and humbly wait to receive God's blessing on your life.

Chapter Thirty-one

Supposing

Let a simple man share a dream and have his say. Supposing Buddha, Allah, Yahweh, and all religious codes come from the same source who breathed His Spirit into the lives of all religious foundations according to culture, creed and nurture; into His prophets, into the life of Christ, His Word made flesh in human form, and finally through the outpouring of his Spirit upon all humanity?

Supposing the words Jesus spoke were inspired by God, and when the world is finally judged, supposing it is not according to the religious codes of behaviour practiced by the individual, but according to how each man and woman has lived their life in relationship to others?

"When the Son of Man comes in His glory and all the angels with Him, He will sit in state on his throne, with all the nations gathered before Him" (Matthew 25:31).

Then supposing all of us, from our various religious platforms cry out "Lord, Lord!" Will we be counted among the sheep or the goats?

Prayer

Lord, make me aware of all your people
And grant me the grace to humbly serve
And be aware of the needs of all men, women and
    children
Of different creeds, colour or culture
Remembering that in serving our fellows,
We serve You.
Amen.

Chapter Thirty-two
The Bible

Some people have to read the Bible and study it in an academic way as part of their job, others see it as a wonderful work of literature, and that it is. One can read it as a novel, and there are many fascinating tales about human beings and the way they behave. You may want to sit and read the Bible from beginning to the end in one go, and find you want to give it up because it seems boring and cruel.

The Bible is a disorderly collection of sixty-odd books written by different people over a period of about three thousand-odd years and has many contradictions and inconsistencies, but wow! If it is read with an interest in human beings, then we see it as a book about life as it really is and includes the sublime and the ridiculous, people who believe and people who do not believe, innocent and guilty, good and bad, those who are full of hope and those who despair.

In a way it is a book about us, but it is also a book about God, therefore, it is a book about our story and why we are here. The Bible is like a window from which we look out to see the expression on the faces of men and women of faith like Abraham and Sarah, for example, who burst out laughing when God tells them he is going to keep his promise and give them the son they always yearned for. We see joy on King David's face as he dances in the nude in front of the ark; Paul struck dumb on the road to Damascus, and the surprise on the face of a younger son who, having spent his father's fortune, comes home to receive a joyful welcome and a magnificent celebration, while his elder brother cannot contain his anger against his father's generosity.

You may even catch a glimpse of your own face in one of the stories and see yourself in a different way and discover you can do things you were previously afraid of doing and may pluck up courage to attempt the impossible!

And finally, if you find yourself getting a little lost on the way, get a bible commentary to help you understand the customs and practices of the society of biblical times. If somehow you manage to see in the Bible a new way of looking at the world, you will discover you are viewing life through the eyes of God, who will speak to you from the depth of your being!

Prayer

Help me to see through your Word made flesh
That man "does not live on bread alone,
But by the word of God".[2]
Amen.

---

[2] Matthew 4:4

Chapter Thirty-three

The Devil

As long as we picture the devil as someone dressed in red with pointed ears, horns, a tail, carrying a fork in his hand, we relegate him to the bogyman of childhood fears; letting the real devil parade freely in the affairs of the world, causing confusion and rebellion. For the devil is an impressive being, he is perspicacious, cunning as a fox and attractive as an angel. He cunningly persuaded Eve, and then helped her to tempt Adam (Genesis 3); and leads us astray as soon as we start speaking lies (Psalms 58:3); therefore, the devil is the father of all lies (John 8:44) and anyone who believes in him (that is, lies) will be kept out of the city gates (Revelation 22:15).

When we take lies seriously we take the devil seriously and see that destroyer in a new light; he leaves us with a bitter taste in our mouth as he distorts relationships and brings disorder in community, the family and the state, both national and international. One only has to look up history books ancient and modern to see his effect. We see his influence in recent world events, such as the debate on the justification for war on Iraq: was the information available doctored to suit its ends? The debate still goes on; and maybe the axis of evil covers the whole globe and not just a handful of named nations.

The devil is a murderer, deceitful and faithless, and cannot be trusted; he has the opposite qualities of truth, which is God; therefore it is impossible for God to lie (Hebrews 6:18) and He is faithful to his promise – Jesus is the fulfilment of the promise made to the fathers (Romans 15:8). To take the devil seriously is to take the view that the total evil in the world is greater than the sum of all its parts; and if we think we are above sin then we deceive ourselves (1 John 1:8). To take the devil seriously is also to take seriously the total freedom we are given and to become aware of our responsibility to love and care for one another. Remember Lucifer was an angel who, even in Paradise, was free to get the hell out of it (Isaiah 14:12).

Chapter Thirty-four

The Graciousness of God

It always comes as a surprise when we learn that God is gracious, especially to the seemingly undeserving. For example, take the criminal who hung on a cross beside Jesus, the one who at the last moment recognised something special about the person beside him who was under the same sentence of death, but for doing nothing wrong (Luke 23:40). He doesn't cry out for forgiveness by confessing his sins or making a display of being sorry. He simply asks: "Jesus, remember me when you come into your kingdom", and Jesus replies: "Today you will be with me in paradise." No penitential rite seems to be required, simply a request from the heart.

Then there is Mary Magdalene, a woman who was in the business of pleasing men for money. She was about to be stoned to death having been caught in the act of her trade; Jesus saves her from a screaming crowd with stones in their hands, ready to perform their ritual requirement of the Jewish law code by challenging the one without sin to cast the first stone. Jesus too does not condemn, but tells her to change her lifestyle, which she does, and follows him. Mary becomes the first person to witness the resurrection and goes to the disciples with the news: "I have seen the Lord!" (John 20)

The graciousness of God seems to have no bounds. Take Peter. He had badly let his best friend down by denying on three separate occasions that he knew Jesus during His time of greatest need (Matthew 26:75). After His resurrection, Jesus still trusts Peter and says to him: "Feed my sheep." What love bestows such grace? Even the doubting Thomas can't escape the gracious love of God and is the first to declare: "My Lord and my God" (John 20:29).

Finally, what about you and me? We are all undeserving creatures falling short of fulfilling the law of love. Nevertheless, we are told that "God loved the world so much that he gave his only son, that everyone who has faith in him may not die but have eternal life" (John 3:16). The graciousness of God transcends all understanding and although "all alike have sinned, and are deprived of the divine splendour" (Romans 3:23) yet we can all be justified and freed by the grace of our Lord Jesus Christ who by the graciousness of God, liberates us and sets us free!

Chapter Thirty-five

The Kingdom of God

The kingdom of God may have more to do with our state of being than an actual place on a map, therefore, do not go looking in an outward direction for you will not find anything and become disappointed. "The kingdom of God is within you" (Luke 17:21) and when Jesus walked the streets of Galilee it was present in his being (Matthew 12:28). Then, when the day of Pentecost arrived (Acts 2), the Holy Spirit was poured out on the world, the kingdom of God was seen within a room filled with believers, and ever since the kingdom is made visible when his followers live in unity with the breaking and sharing of bread and the way they love one another.

The kingdom of God is made visible here on earth, not as a geographical location, but residing in the heart of a believer; nevertheless, it has only partially come on earth and can be seen in various and odd ways among us. Jesus gave us the best picture of locating the kingdom of heaven and likened it to a merchant looking for the finest pearl (Matthew 13:46) and the prodigal came to discover it for himself the hard way; having gone looking all over the place for his treasure, he found it was located in his heart. On returning home, where his heart found the joy he sought, was rewarded as a true son of his father.

See my section on prayer and invite the Holy Spirit into your life and discover the wonder of the kingdom of God for yourself.

Chapter Thirty-six

There's No Fool Like God's Fool

"The fool has said in his heart, there is no God" (Psalms 14:1).

In general, people seem to favour the wisdom of the worldly-wise, and there is much to be said for the advancements made in science and technology, which helps give us the "good life". But it doesn't guarantee personality-enhancing change, making us more human and tolerant of others; rather, it helps us become more subtle in being dishonest, ruthless and indifferent towards others; a kind of intelligent "bad manners". The creative wealth of the worldly-wise – which is transient and apt to be stolen, lost or to decay – cannot save us from death, purchase our ransom from God or redeem our soul; "for wise men perish the same way as the fool; they both die" (Psalms 49).

There is another kind of fool: "fools for Christ" (1 Corinthians 4:10): those who lose their lives for Christ; become God's fools. For the cross of Christ is seen as folly to the worldly-wise and their subtle debates, but it is the very power of God (1 Corinthians 18). God has taken what the world calls weakness and shown that sacrificial love is capable of overturning the fortunes of the world. It is the Spirit of God, exploring the depth of our being that changes human hearts; if humanity can relegate the wisdom and learning of the world, for that too is good, and place it below the authority of God's wisdom, then indeed we may have "heaven on earth".

Prayer

Father, grant me the gift of wisdom
That I may know your ways,
Understand your word and do your will,
Through Jesus Christ our Lord.
Amen.

Chapter Thirty-seven

Trinity

For St Ireanaeus, the Incarnation was a sign of joining the end to the beginning; that is, to unite humanity back with God, restoring to humanity what was lost through the fall (Genesis 3). Consequently, the Incarnation has had a radical effect upon human nature, enabling human beings to share in the divinity through Christ. Through Christ's life, death and resurrection and the sending of the Holy Spirit, humanity once again has the opportunity to be joined to God in a Trinitarian relationship of Father, Son and Holy Spirit. This is "life everlasting", a life quickened by the Holy Spirit of God, which brings us into fellowship with Christ, incorporating us into his body; we share his eternal life in the presence of God.

This is not just a heavenly reality; it is costly as it places us in a new relationship with the created order where we are re-installed as "our brother's keeper" and have to work to take care of the environment and for love, justice, and mercy for all people. Christ heals because he is the embodiment of God's love and working through his body church, he extends the Incarnation through faithful humanity to reflect love, joy, peace and healing.

"In the beginning was the Word, the Word was with God, and the Word was God. The Word became flesh and dwelt among us" (John 1:1).

Prayer

God the Father, I adore you,
God the Son, I adore you,
God the Holy Spirit, I adore you.
Come dwell in me Holy Trinity;
Father, Son and Holy Spirit.
Amen.

Chapter Thirty-eight

Truth

When Pilate asked: "What is truth"? (John 18:38), he asked the eternal and seemingly unanswerable question that the power of state cannot define, for eternal truth seems to reside outside the sphere of earthly understanding.

Maybe the only inkling we perceive of truth in the affairs of the world is when:

> Mercy and truth have met together;
> Righteousness and peace have kissed.
> Truth shall spring out of the earth,
> And righteousness shall look down from heaven.
>
> Psalms 85:10–11

Lord, amidst the abundance of knowledge, hypotheses, and variety of choice, I find it is difficult to know what is the truth. Help and guide me to see in you the Way, the Truth and the Life.

Prayer

> "Praise, the Lord, all you Gentiles!
> Laud Him, all you people!
> For His merciful kindness is great towards us,
> And the truth of the Lord endures for ever."
>
> *Psalms 117*

Chapter Thirty-nine

Natural Phenomena

As part of creation, our human nature can be just as destructive and unpredictable as a tsunami: looking all calm and innocent on the surface, while beneath the subconscious stir deep emotions that are likely to erupt into an outburst of uncontrollable aggression at the drop of a hat.

Then, like a tsunami, a breakdown of values can cause an eruption of mind, body and spirit that sends tidal waves of destruction, which affect a wide area of relationships. These are not acts of God, but natural phenomena of a living organism continually in the flux of death and rebirth; belief and unbelief; lies and truth; of earth and spirit; war and peace; justice and injustice; good and bad; till the time is ripe and the consciousness of the world erupts like a tsunami. Then there will be a violent earthquake and the sky fall into the sea, like figs shaken in the wind (Revelation 6:12).

Prayer

Lord, how many times have we been warned
Of the unruly and wild nature of humanity
Which walks the way of the world and lives like a
    wild beast;
Exploiting justice and not showing mercy to the
    poor in spirit,
And, through the strength of arms or terror,
Destroys the world You have created through the
    spilling of blood?
Have mercy upon us O Lord,
And forgive our foolish ways,
As we pray for Your world without end.
Amen.

Chapter Forty

Wealth

There is something about the rich man that attracts Jesus, but Jesus puts an unfair challenge before him by asking him to sell all his possessions as a precondition for entering the kingdom of God. If we link this to an earlier passage about the kingdom belonging to innocents – young children – then we may see things differently. Perhaps to be part of God's kingdom we need to acknowledge God as Father and that is not something we achieve by ourselves, but by grace. Maybe the story is not after all about wealth, but about our relationship with God, and if our possessions get in the way, preventing us from seeing the wood from the trees, it distorts our relationship with God. Maybe the person asking the question about eternal life was more beholden to his possessions than the eternal life he was seeking, and perhaps the story after all was not about wealth, but about not letting our possessions get in the way of our relationship with God.

"One thing you lack: go, sell everything you have, and come, follow me" (Mark 10:21).

Prayer

Lord, help me to treat wealth
As a gift from heaven to spend on earth,
But to know when to let go of the earthly things
And follow in your footsteps.
Amen.

Chapter Forty-one

Worry

Worry can destroy our peace and a worried person is someone who could find him or herself at war within; this conflict within can become the cause of much disease.

Its symptoms can find us waking up tired after sleepless nights, and cause us to see problems lurking in every corner. We are told that many illnesses may have their root in stress, caused by worry and it can shorten our life expectancy. One thing is certain: we cannot stop worrying by worrying! A non-medical cure may be talking to a trusted friend and sharing our troubles; a good listener may be worth a thousand pills.

Failing that, find time to sit down and think on this.

Jesus said: "Come to me all whose work is hard, whose load is heavy, and your souls will find relief" (Matthew 11:28).

"Can any of you for all your worrying, add one single day to your span of life? So do not worry about tomorrow; each day has enough trouble of its own" (Matthew 6: 19–34).

Prayer

Lord, I find it difficult to stop worrying
When things do not go according to plan and I get
    things wrong.
When everyone seems to doubt my ability
To achieve the goals that confront me in life,
And even I start doubting my own ability.
Lord, during these times,
Carry me on your shoulder and ease the burden
Till I am strong enough to walk on my own once again
With you beside me.
Amen.

Chapter Forty-two

XYZ, Storytellers

Storytellers are imaginative thinkers, who explore, ponder and hypothesise on the nature of being, then endeavour to communicate the result of their search for meaning. Storytelling has encouraged primitive art, oral tradition, the Bible, Koran and *Bhagavad-Gita*, mathematical formula dealing with fixed laws in nature as well as the discovery by quantum physicists that nature can be like a game of dice.

Scientists have become the new storytellers – telling stories about DNA, the Big Bang of creation, scientific and political ideologies and about globalisation – while continuing to investigate the meaning of consciousness and what makes humankind special.

Although exploration for meaning has moved from primitive to sophisticated, we still search for a solution to the dilemma of connecting consciousness, mind and matter. Perhaps something more than science is required to unite body and soul, for science may be able to care for the body – that is evident from our improved standard of living – but what about the soul of humankind? Is this beyond science, and is it something to do with God, who "breathed into his nostrils the breath of life, and man became a living soul" (Genesis 2:7)? And is this why Jesus said: "Fear Him who is able to destroy both soul and body" (Matthew 10:28).

In all the stories ever told, in those that are being told now and those that will be told in the future, one thing remains constant, be it told religiously, politically, scientifically, psychologically or ideologically: there is one continuous battle raging around us, and that is the *battle to control our minds*! "For God knows that in the day you eat of it, your eyes will be opened and you will be like God, knowing good and evil" (Genesis 3:5).

Printed in the United Kingdom
by Lightning Source UK Ltd.
119134UK00001B/47